OUR EARTH IN ACTION

EARTHQUAKES

Chris Oxlade

W
FRANKLIN WATTS

This edition published 2014 by Franklin Watts

Copyright © 2014 Franklin Watts

Franklin Watts
338 Euston Road
London NW1 3BH

Franklin Watts Australia
Level 17/207 Kent Street
Sydney, NSW 2000

A CIP catalogue record for this book is available
from the British Library.

Dewey number: 551.22

ISBN 978 1 4451 3199 3

Printed in China

Franklin Watts is a division of Hachette Children's Books,
an Hachette UK company.
www.hachette.co.uk

Artwork: John Alston
Editor: Sarah Ridley
Design: Thomas Keenes
Editor in Chief: John C. Miles
Art director: Jonathan Hair

Picture credits:
Tom Bean/Corbis: front cover, 1. James Benet/istockphoto: 23. Paula Bronstein/Getty Images: 26tr. China Photos/Getty Images: 5. James King Holmes/SPL: 22. Image Bank/Getty Images: 28b, 29. INOONG/AFP/Getty Images: 15. Jiji Press/AFP/Getty Images: 17b. Chung Sung-Jun/Getty Images: 18. Banaras Khan/AFP/Getty Images: 27. Masanori Kobayashi/Alamy: 12. Uyen Li /Getty Images: 20. Tim McCraig/istockphoto: 14. Dario Mitidieri/Reportage/Getty Images: 16. Chuck Nacke/Time & Life/Getty Images: 17t. Reportage/Getty Images: 25. Roger Ressmeyer/Corbis: 21. Yali Shi/istockphoto: 4. Orlando Sierra/AFP/Getty Images: 13. George Steinmetz/SPL: 9. Stone/Getty Images: 6. Topical Press/Hulton Archive/Getty Images: 19. Natsuko Utsumi/Liaison/Getty Images: 24b. Peeter Viisimaa/istockphoto: 11. Every attempt has been made to clear copyright. Should there be any inadvertent omission please apply to the publisher for rectification.

CONTENTS

ABOUT EARTHQUAKES

Put simply, an earthquake is a shaking movement of the ground. It can be a slight tremor or a violent juddering. Earthquakes are caused by sudden movements of rocks inside the Earth. They are destructive events – they can rip open the Earth's surface and destroy buildings. Scientists detect about half a million earthquakes each year, but only about a hundred of these are powerful enough to do any damage.

DURING AN EARTHQUAKE

An earthquake is set off when two bodies of rock that are rubbing against each other slip suddenly. The movement makes the rocks vibrate, sending out shock waves. Where the waves reach the surface, they make it shake up and down, move from side to side and roll about. During a powerful earthquake, there is generally a sudden jolt of the ground, followed by strong shaking and a rumbling noise. There are often aftershocks (smaller earthquakes) after the main earthquake, caused by the rocks settling down again. Scientists study how and why earthquakes happen, but they can't predict accurately when they will happen.

EARTHQUAKE EFFECTS

Powerful earthquakes change the Earth's surface by cracking it, lifting it, dropping it and setting off landslides and tsunamis. The shaking on the surface is very destructive for buildings and other structures, such as roads, bridges and dams. Even the largest and most solid-looking buildings can collapse. Most earthquake victims are trapped in collapsed buildings, or hit

▼ A road surface broken into pieces by up and down movements of the ground beneath during an earthquake.

▲ *Earthquakes cause buildings to collapse and other types of widespread devastation.*

by them as they collapse. The death toll is highest when earthquakes happen during the daytime, with offices, schools and other large buildings packed with people. Earthquakes also damage vital services, such as water supplies, electricity supplies and transport. Broken gas mains can lead to fires. Normal life is completely disrupted, and may take months or years to return to normal.

Deadly earthquakes

Earthquakes are one of the most deadly natural hazards. On average, they kill 10,000 people each year (but many more in some years and many fewer in other years). In recent history, one of the most deadly earthquakes on record happened in Tangshan, China, in 1976. Official figures state that more than 240,000 people were killed – but it may have been a much higher figure, more like 600,000.

PLATE TECTONICS

Earthquakes happen because of the internal structure of the Earth. The movement of semi-molten rocks deep inside the Earth causes parts of the Earth's crust (its outer layer) to distort and eventually break. Each time a new break, or fault, appears, an earthquake occurs.

THE EARTH'S INSIDES

The Earth has four main layers, each with different properties. At the centre are the inner core and outer core, made mostly from iron. Next comes the mantle, made from hot, rocky material. The Earth's outer layer is the crust. It is very thin compared to the other layers – less than 100 km thick everywhere and as little as 6 km thick under the oceans. The crust, together with the very top layer of the mantle, forms a layer called the lithosphere.

A CRACKED CRUST

The Earth's lithosphere is cracked into about a dozen giant pieces called tectonic plates. They move around the Earth's surface at speeds of only a few centimetres a year. The movement of the Earth's continents on their tectonic plates is known as continental drift.

PLATE BOUNDARIES

The lines formed where plates meet each other are called plate boundaries. There are three types – constructive, destructive and conservative. At a constructive boundary the two plates move apart and new rock fills the gap. At a destructive boundary, the two plates move towards each other, and the rocks in the plates are crushed together. At a conservative boundary, the two plates slide past each other in opposite directions.

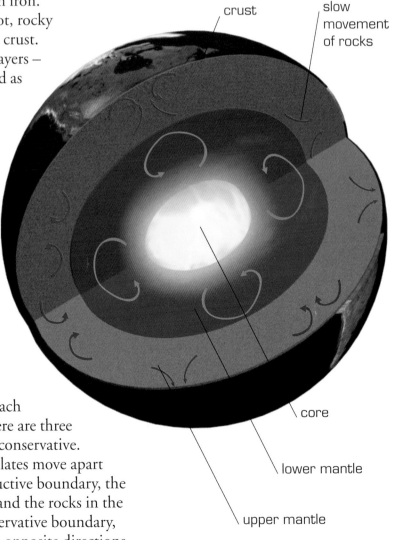

▼ *The internal layers of the Earth. Slow movement of rocks makes tectonic plates move, causing earthquakes.*

crust

slow movement of rocks

core

lower mantle

upper mantle

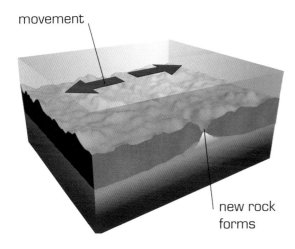

▲ *A constructive plate boundary. The tectonic plates are moving slowly apart.*

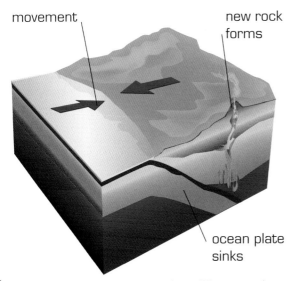

▲ *A destructive plate boundary. The two plates are moving towards each other.*

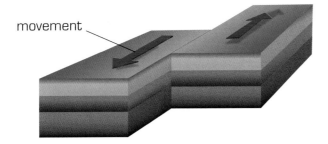

▲ *A conservative plate boundary. The two plates are moving past each other.*

Faults

The movement of plates at boundaries causes rock at the edges of the plates to be stretched, crushed and cracked. The cracks are called faults. They can be many kilometres long and deep. Earthquakes happen when cracks first form, and when the rock on each side of a fault slips suddenly. The rocks on the two sides of the fault can move up, down or sideways.

▼ *The San Andreas fault, California.*

WHERE EARTHQUAKES HAPPEN

A quick study of where earthquakes happen reveals that most occur along the boundaries between the Earth's tectonic plates. Because the plates move relative to each other, rocks along faults in the edges of the plates must also gradually move.

Sometimes friction prevents these movements from happening smoothly. Instead, the plates get locked together and pressure builds up until the plates suddenly move on, releasing the stored energy and causing an earthquake.

SHALLOW AND DEEP

The place in a fault where an earthquake is set off is called the earthquake's focus or hypocentre. The focus can be anything from a few kilometres to hundreds of kilometres underground, but in most earthquakes it is less than 30 km below ground. Deep earthquakes, even when very powerful, do less damage than shallow earthquakes because their energy spreads out before it reaches the surface.

BOUNDARY EARTHQUAKES

Powerful earthquakes happen at destructive boundaries and conservative boundaries. At destructive boundaries, the plate that sinks

▼ Earthquakes are linked to tectonic plate boundaries. The red lines on this map mark the boundaries of the Earth's tectonic plates.

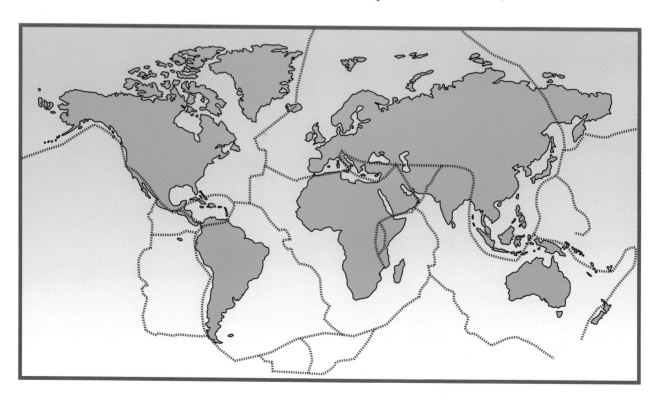

More causes of earthquakes

Volcanic eruptions also cause earthquakes. Movement of magma underground sets off swarms of earthquakes before an eruption. An explosive eruption causes earthquakes as gas and ash are blasted into the air. Human activities, such as mining and drilling for oil, often set off small earthquakes because they change the forces on rocks.

▼ *Volcanologists study a volcano.*

down into the mantle becomes stressed and then cracks, causing earthquakes. Here, earthquakes can be shallow or deep. Earthquakes in Alaska and the Himalayas are destructive boundary earthquakes. At conservative boundaries the action of the plates sliding past each other rips the edges of the plates, creating faults. Shallow earthquakes are set off when the faults slip suddenly. Earthquakes in California, USA, are conservative boundary earthquakes. Earthquakes also happen at constructive boundaries as new crust cracks, but these tend to be small.

INTRAPLATE EARTHQUAKES

There are sometimes faults in a tectonic plate far from its boundaries, caused by rock movements millions of years ago. Sudden movements of these faults cause 'intraplate' earthquakes. They are often unexpected because nobody knows the faults are there beforehand.

EARTHQUAKE WAVES

You can think of an earthquake as a sudden release of energy underground. The energy spreads out from the focus in waves (called seismic waves) that travel through the rock in the Earth's crust. The waves make rocks vibrate in different directions as they pass. The further the waves travel from the epicentre, the weaker they become.

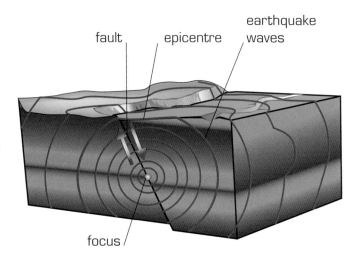

TYPES OF SEISMIC WAVES

There are three main types of seismic wave – primary, secondary and surface. Primary (P) waves compress and expand rock as they pass (like compressions moving along a slinky spring). On average, they travel at about 8 km per second. Secondary (S) waves make the rock move from side-to-side or up and down (like waves on a string shaken at one end). On average they travel at about 5 km per second. Surface waves are caused by P and S waves arriving at the surface. They spread out from the epicentre causing shaking and rolling of the surface. They travel slightly slower than P and S waves. P and S waves do most damage close to the epicentre of an earthquake. Surface waves do most damage at large distances from the epicentre.

▲ An earthquake set off by a slip in a fault. One block moves up and the other down. The epicentre is the point on the surface directly above the focus.

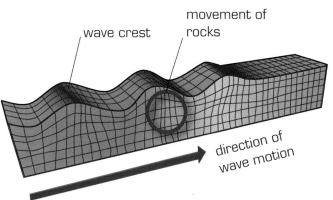

▲ Surface waves make rocks move in circles as they pass, forcing the surface up and down.

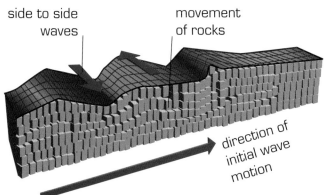

▲ Secondary waves shake rock from side to side as they pass.

MEASURING EARTHQUAKES

Scientists measure the size of earthquakes in various ways. Magnitude is a measure of the size of earthquake waves. The most well-known magnitude scale is the Richter scale, named after its inventor, Charles Richter. On this scale, 1 is a very minor earthquake, and 9 is a very major earthquake. Since Richter, earthquake scientists have developed a different measurement, called moment magnitude, which is a more accurate reflection of an earthquake's energy. This is calculated from the area of the fault that moves and how far it moves. On both types of scale, an increase in one on the scale shows an increase of ten times in magnitude.

Earthquake intensity

Intensity is a measure of the shaking of the ground at a particular place on the surface. It is estimated from the effects of the shaking. For example, on the Mercalli Intensity Scale, 6 means slight damage to buildings, and 11 means most buildings are destroyed. Intensity becomes lower further from the epicentre of an earthquake because the earthquake's energy spreads out.

▼ *Buildings reduced to rubble by violent movements of the ground as earthquake waves passed by.*

EFFECTS ON THE LANDSCAPE

Earthquakes have various effects on the landscape. As well as the shaking caused as earthquake waves pass by, the shaking leaves cracks in the surface, and can set off landslides and avalanches. When a fault moves, the ground can be raised or lowered, sometimes by many metres.

▼ *Cracks in the ground are common as the earth is ripped apart by earthquake waves.*

SURFACE SLIPS

Where a fault reaches the surface, the movement that sets off an earthquake rips the surface. This forms a surface feature called a slip. Sideways slips make rips along the surface. Up and down slips leave steps in the surface. The slips range in size from a few centimetres to many metres.

▲ *A slip moves the ground sideways at a strike-slip fault.*

▲ *A slip moves the ground up and down at a normal fault.*

LANDSLIDES

A landslide happens when a block of soil or rock becomes detached from a hillside or cliff and slides to the bottom. Landslides happen where the soil or rock on a slope is already unstable. The instability can be caused by erosion at the base of the slope (by a river or waves) or by people cutting into the slope, perhaps to make a road. Earthquake shaking can also set off rock falls. In turn, landslides can set off tsunamis (see pages 14-15) and cause floods by blocking rivers.

EARTHQUAKE AVALANCHES

An avalanche is a body of snow sliding down a hillside. It happens where a layer of snow begins to slide on the snow underneath. An avalanche travels at hundreds of kilometres per hour, and sweeps away anything in its path. Avalanches are often set off by earthquakes when shaking releases a layer of snow. The most devastating earthquake-induced avalanche we know about happened in 1970. A strong earthquake under the Pacific Ocean set off an avalanche on a mountain called Huascaran in the Peruvian Andes. Snow hurtled 4 km down the mountainside at about 280 km per hour, sweeping rock and mud with it. It buried the town of Yungay under 10 m of snow, ice and rubble, killing 50,000 people.

▲ *This mudslide in El Salvador was set off by an earthquake in 2001. Hundreds of people were buried.*

Mudslides

When earthquake waves travel through wet soil, the soil behaves in a peculiar way. It becomes liquefied, which means it behaves like a liquid instead of a solid. You see a similar effect when you wiggle your foot on wet sand. Liquefaction can lead to mudslides, where wet soil flows downhill, and also fountains, where underground water comes to the surface.

TSUNAMIS

A tsunami is a wave that travels across a sea or ocean. Most tsunamis are set off by earthquakes under the ocean. Large tsunamis do a great deal of damage when they hit low-lying coasts. A tsunami is not the same as a tidal wave, which is a wave set off by a rising tide.

CAUSING TSUNAMIS

An earthquake under the ocean can make the sea floor rise or fall suddenly. This causes all the water above to be lifted or dropped, which makes the ocean surface rise or fall. This movement sets off a wave that spreads out in all directions, like the ripples from a stone thrown into a pond. In the deep ocean, the wave measures many kilometres from its trough to its peak, and may be only a metre high. It travels at extremely high speeds (up to 900 km per hour). The trouble begins when a tsunami reaches shallow water. It slows, becomes shorter and higher. At this point, a powerful tsunami can reach 30 m above normal sea level. Some tsunamis are set off by landslides on coasts, or on undersea slopes, themselves caused by earthquakes.

THE 2004 ASIAN TSUNAMI

The worst natural disaster of recent times was the Asian tsunami of 2004. The tsunami was set off by the Great Sumatra-Andaman earthquake, the third strongest earthquake ever recorded,

▼ *Waves from the Great Sumatra-Andaman earthquake spread right across the Indian Ocean.*

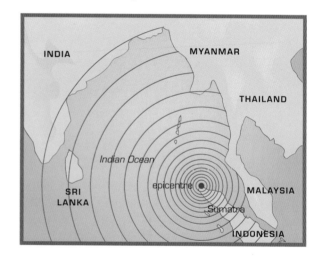

INDIA · MYANMAR · THAILAND · SRI LANKA · Indian Ocean · epicentre · Sumatra · MALAYSIA · INDONESIA

Tsunami warnings

TSUNAMI HAZARD ZONE

IN CASE OF EARTHQUAKE GO TO HIGH GROUND OR INLAND

Millions of people living in low-lying coastal areas are at risk from tsunamis. The Asian tsunami of 2004 showed just how great these risks are, especially when there is no warning. Japan has suffered many tsunami disasters, and has led the way in setting up a tsunami warning system in the Pacific Ocean. Seismic monitoring stations and mid-ocean buoys aim to track and predict tsunamis. A similar system now operates in the Indian Ocean.

with a magnitude of 9.1–9.3. The epicentre was in the sea off the island of Sumatra in Indonesia, and the cause was rock movement in a destructive boundary. The tsunami devastated the coastlines of Indonesia and Thailand, and hours later, inflicted similar damage on certain coastlines in Sri Lanka and India. More than 225,000 people were killed, and whole coastal communities were destroyed.

▲ *The tsunami produced by the 2004 earthquake created a trail of devastation that wiped out entire communities around the Indian Ocean.*

EFFECTS ON BUILDINGS

Even the most powerful earthquakes are not particularly dangerous for people who are out in the open. The majority of earthquake victims are killed or injured inside falling buildings. Most damage is done when buildings are shaken to pieces by earthquake waves. Earthquakes also damage other structures, such as roads and railways, bridges and tunnels, and infrastructure such as water pipes and gas mains.

BUILDING TYPES

Many people think that a tall building is the most dangerous place to be in an earthquake. In fact, tall buildings often survive when low-rise buildings are badly damaged. It just depends on the frequency and direction of the shaking. However, high-rise buildings can hit each other as they sway. In general, buildings that are strong but flexible survive best. This includes steel-framed skyscrapers and wooden-framed houses. Buildings made from bricks or stones that are not well cemented together tend to collapse.

▼ A partially collapsed office building. Its frame has broken in an earthquake.

Ground types

The quality of the ground under a building is as important as the quality of the building itself. Soft ground tends to amplify seismic waves, creating more damage, so building on solid rock is safest. Waterlogged ground is the worst type of ground. During an earthquake it can undergo liquefaction (see page 13), which allows building foundations to sink into it.

▲ *The supporting columns of expressways can give way during earthquakes if they are not designed properly.*

▼ *Buildings are often reduced to a heap of rubble, making the task of search and rescue extremely difficult.*

Buildings made from concrete slabs and columns, where the slabs and columns are not joined together strongly, are also at high risk.

Most buildings collapse because they are not designed to withstand earthquakes. This may be because a major earthquake has never struck before in a particular area, because building regulations are not strict enough (or are ignored) or because people cannot afford to follow the regulations. In 1988, an earthquake hit the Armenian town of Leninakan, where 80% of the buildings, which were made from poorly joined concrete slabs, collapsed.

BUILDING HAZARDS

The greatest danger in a collapsing building is being trapped between heavy concrete floors or under piles of rubble. It can take days for rescuers to search a collapsed building, which is often too late for people who have survived the collapse. Inside, people are also in danger from falling furniture and burst pipes. In the streets, hazards include collapsing walls, falling roof tiles and chimneys, flying glass and rubble.

LIVING WITH EARTHQUAKES

Hundreds of millions of people live in places at risk from earthquakes. They include the populations of huge cities, such as Tokyo and Los Angeles. In many earthquake zones, there are disaster plans in place so that the authorities and emergency services can respond quickly. People are also educated on how to prepare and protect themselves.

EARTHQUAKE PLANNING

A major earthquake is capable of destroying or disrupting everything that people rely on – their homes, services (such as fuel and fresh water supplies), transport, shops, banks and schools. Disaster plans must take this into consideration. Emergency responses include search and rescue, reserves of medical equipment at hospitals, temporary shelter, providing food and water supplies, and in the long term, checking the safety of buildings and reconstruction. Earthquake hazard maps are drawn up by scientists. They show which areas of a town or city are most at risk because of soft ground, landslides or tsunamis. Important buildings,

▼ Children who live in earthquake zones regularly practise their earthquake drills.

Earthquake protection in Japan

Japan has learned from a history of catastrophic earthquakes, such as the Great Kanto earthquake of 1923, which wrecked Tokyo, killing up to 143,000 people. New Japanese buildings are earthquake resistant. People also keep emergency supplies and equipment to hand and practise earthquake drills at school and at work. The high-speed Bullet trains have a seismic warning system that shuts off power in an earthquake.

▶ *Tokyo after the 1923 earthquake.*

such as hospitals and fire stations, are placed in the safer areas, so that disruption is less likely during an earthquake.

EARTHQUAKE ADVICE

In earthquake zones the authorities attempt to educate people about the hazards. There is advice about how to prepare for earthquakes, and what to do during an earthquake and immediately afterwards. Preparing for an earthquake includes gathering together an emergency kit (containing water, food, a radio, spare batteries, cooking equipment and so on) and attaching heavy furniture to walls. During an earthquake, people already indoors are advised to stay indoors, get under a strong table and hold tight (this is known as 'duck, cover and hold'). People already outdoors are advised to stay away from buildings, and away from the seashore, where tsunamis might hit.

During an earthquake:

Do

- duck, cover and hold — quickly get under a table, hold on and cover your eyes
- stay away from tall, heavy furniture and windows, which could topple or smash
- if you are in bed, stay there with a pillow over your head
- if you are outside, find a space away from buildings and trees, and sit down
- if you are in a car, drive away from buildings, stop and stay in the car

And don't

- panic and run about
- run into a building or out of a building
- stand under a doorway (a doorway is not a strong place)
- worry if alarms and sprinklers go off around you
- forget where your emergency kit is
- forget that there might be aftershocks soon after the main earthquake

BUILDING FOR EARTHQUAKES

Because collapsing buildings are one of the greatest hazards of earthquakes, it is important that buildings in earthquake zones are earthquake proof. A great deal of research goes into the design of earthquake-proof buildings. Earthquake proofing is especially important for buildings where collapse would be catastrophic, such as nuclear power stations.

BUILDING MOVEMENT

During an earthquake, a building can be shaken in many different directions, including up and down. It can also be shaken at different frequencies – from many times a second to once every few seconds. Buildings respond differently to different patterns of shaking. A high-rise building may hardly move in one earthquake, but sway violently in another.

IMPORTANT FOUNDATIONS

Foundations support a building on the ground. They spread the weight of the building (and everything inside) into the ground so that the ground does not subside. Foundations on solid rock are best, as the building is connected directly to the rock. Slab foundations work on soft ground, but soft ground can liquefy during an earthquake, so that the foundations sink.

◄ *The bottom-heavy Transamerica Pyramid in San Francisco is unlikely to topple in an earthquake.*

Building isolation

One way of protecting high-rise buildings is isolation. This is separating a building from the ground so that the shaking cannot pass into the building. One method is to use sliding pads between a building's frame and its foundations. Giant springs prevent the building from sliding too far. Another method is active seismic control, which uses computer-controlled pistons to push and pull a building to counteract shaking.

▼ *Testing a model building on a vibrating bed.*

BUILDING DESIGN

In general, buildings that are flexible but strong are best in earthquake zones. Steel-framed buildings are flexible and can even be distorted without collapsing. Concrete frames are also acceptable, but the joints between the floors and columns must be reinforced with large amounts of steel. High-rise buildings must be well separated to prevent them from clashing as they sway. Making the lower floors of a high-rise building stronger and wider makes it more earthquake resistant. In low-rise buildings, wooden frames resist shaking well and putting a strong metal band around a brick or stone house can hold it together. Other structures, such as bridges and dams, must also be earthquake proof.

EARTHQUAKE SCIENCE

The science of earthquakes is called seismology. Seismologists study the internal structure of the Earth (such as tectonic plates and faults), and observe and record what happens to the ground before, during and after earthquakes. They try to predict when earthquakes will strike.

TOOLS OF THE TRADE

The main tool of the seismologist is the seismometer (or seismograph), which detects ground movements. Modern seismometers are extremely sensitive, and can detect shaking that people can't feel. Seismometers are placed in the ground and attached to the rock so that they can pick up seismic waves. Modern devices are digital. They record data or are linked to computers. Remote seismometers send data back to base by radio. Other instruments for seismology include tiltmeters to measure changes in ground level, extensionmeters to measure the movement of faults, and strain gauges to measure the forces on rocks.

Waves inside the Earth

Strong seismic waves from an earthquake travel right through the Earth and are detected on the surface the other side. On the way, they are blocked or bent by the different layers of the Earth. Studying how seismic waves travel through the Earth has allowed seismologists to work out the internal structure of the Earth.

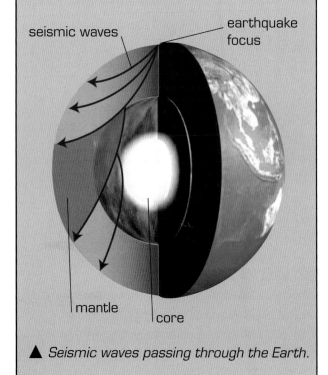

seismic waves

earthquake focus

mantle

core

▲ *Seismic waves passing through the Earth.*

◄ *This scientist is deploying a remote seismometer in a field to measure seismic waves in the ground beneath.*

FINDING THE FOCUS

By studying when different waves (P waves, S waves and surface waves) from an earthquake arrive at different seismometers, seismologists can calculate where the earthquake originated (i.e. where its focus was). It is important to locate where new faults have begun, or where old faults have moved again.

PREDICTING EARTHQUAKES

We can't stop earthquakes happening but if we could predict them, we could save thousands of lives. However, despite the fact that we know a great deal about earthquakes, predicting them is almost impossible. By studying previous earthquakes at a place, seismologists can give a probability of another earthquake happening on a particular day, month, or year. But they can't say for certain that an earthquake will happen at a particular time. In 1975, seismologists predicted the Haicheng-Yingkou earthquake in China, and thousands of people were evacuated before it struck. In this case, there were many foreshocks – small tremors – which showed an earthquake was probably coming. Unfortunately, most earthquakes are not preceded by foreshocks.

▲ *Seismic waves being recorded on paper drums.*

CASE STUDY: KOBE 1995

Kobe is a Japanese city with a population of 1.5 million people. In the morning of 17 January 1995, Kobe was hit by an earthquake now known as the Great Hanshin earthquake or Kobe earthquake. It was Japan's worst earthquake for more than 70 years and showed that even a modern city can be badly affected by a powerful earthquake.

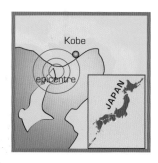

▲ Location map of Kobe and epicentre.

CAUSES OF THE QUAKE

The Great Hanshin earthquake was caused by a fault close to a destructive plate boundary. It measured 6.9 on the Richter scale. The focus was just 16 km underground and the epicentre just 20 km from Kobe, which is why the intensity of the shaking in Kobe was so strong. Surface movements measured 18 cm from side to side and 12 cm up and down. The main earthquake was followed by thousands of aftershocks.

▶ The top deck of one of Kobe's expressways toppled sideways when its supporting columns crumbled.

THE EFFECTS

Tens of thousands of buildings collapsed or were damaged so badly that they had to be demolished. Many traditionally built homes collapsed because their wooden frames could not support their heavy roofs. High-rise buildings collapsed because their concrete slabs or masonry walls were poorly reinforced. A section of motorway a kilometre in length toppled over, and other main roads and bridges were damaged. Two-thirds of the region's railways had to close, including the high-speed Bullet train line. Kobe's busy docks were almost completely wrecked. The greatest problem was fire, caused by broken gas mains setting light to wooden buildings.

▼ A burnt-out building in Kobe. Fires broke out all over the city after the earthquake.

THE AFTERMATH

Nearly 6,500 people died in collapsing buildings and roadways, and in the fires that followed. A further 20,000 people were injured. About 300,000 people lost their homes. Economically, the Great Hanshin earthquake is said to have cost Japan 200 billion US dollars, making it the most expensive natural disaster to hit a single country.

Kobe failures

The disaster in Kobe showed that Japan was not as prepared for a major earthquake as was thought. Fire-fighting was hampered because of damaged water mains, and rescue was slowed by damage to transport routes. The city's hospitals were overwhelmed. There was no warning, and scientists and engineers were surprised by the extent of the damage. Emergency planning has been revised throughout Japan since Kobe.

CASE STUDY: KASHMIR 2005

Kashmir is a mountainous region in northern Pakistan and India. On the morning of 8 October 2005, an earthquake struck in Pakistan-administered Kashmir. It left more than 80,000 dead and millions homeless. The remoteness of the area badly affected the rescue effort.

▲ *Location map showing the epicentre of the Kashmir quake.*

THE EARTHQUAKE

Kashmir lies over a destructive plate boundary between the Eurasian tectonic plate and the Indian tectonic plate. Over millions of years, the collision between these plates has pushed up the Himalayan mountains. The Kashmir earthquake measured 7.6 on the moment magnitude scale. Measurements have shown that the ground level around the epicentre was raised several metres. Hundreds of aftershocks followed, some as powerful as magnitude 6.2.

▲ *Near the epicentre nearly all buildings collapsed.*

▶ *Victims who lost their homes in the Kashmir earthquake living in tented villages.*

EARTHQUAKE EFFECTS

The earthquake devastated the area of Kashmir around the epicentre. Whole villages and towns were destroyed. In the town of Muzaffarabad, 20 km from the epicentre, 80% of buildings collapsed. Stone-built and brick-built homes were shaken to pieces. Multi-storey concrete buildings collapsed like packs of cards. Some of the worst scenes of destruction were at schools and colleges, where thousands of children and students became trapped. Damage spread as far as India and Afghanistan, and the city of Islamabad, 100 km away. The earthquake set off hundreds of landslides on the steep hillsides of the area.

RESCUE EFFORTS

Roads blocked by landslides made it impossible for rescuers to reach remote towns and villages, where hundreds of thousands of people were dead, injured or homeless. The situation was made worse by the approaching winter. People had to fend for themselves for weeks without food and shelter. Eventually, the Pakistan army and international aid teams arrived, bringing medical supplies, food and tents. Helicopters carried aid in and the injured out. The border between Pakistan and India is disputed in Kashmir, but it was opened to allow aid to reach the affected area.

A long-lasting disaster

A year after the earthquake, it was estimated that nearly two million people were still living in tented villages in Kashmir, and had to live through another winter without proper shelter. Years later, rebuilding is still not completed. This shows the problems that earthquakes bring to poor areas of the developing world, where people may lose everything they own and cannot afford to help themselves.

CASE STUDY: SAN FRANCISCO

San Francisco, on the west coast of the USA, lies a few kilometres from a huge fault known as the San Andreas fault. San Francisco has suffered from powerful earthquakes in the past. Scientists think that another – perhaps of magnitude 8 and known as the 'Big One' – is due soon.

▲ *Location map of southern California, showing the San Andreas fault.*

THE SAN ANDREAS FAULT

The boundary between two giant tectonic plates runs down the west coast of the USA. This is a conservative plate boundary. The Pacific plate is moving north-west and the North American plate south-east, passing each other at the rate of about 5 cm per year. The movement has ripped the edges of the plates, creating faults which set off tens of thousands of earthquakes here each year. The largest fault is the 1,100-km-long San Andreas fault that runs close to the coast of California.

▶ *San Francisco is a city of 800,000 people. About 7 million people live in the San Francisco Bay Area.*

THE 1906 EARTHQUAKE

An earthquake of magnitude 8.3 on the Richter scale hit San Francisco on 18 April 1906. It was caused by a sudden jolt along a 400-km length of the San Andreas fault. At the time, most of the city's buildings were made of wood. Many survived the shaking, but were destroyed by fire. Some masonry buildings collapsed, as did many buildings built on soft ground near the waterfront. About 300,000 people were made homeless, but luckily only about 700 were killed. Another strong earthquake, measuring 6.9 on the Richter scale, hit San Francisco in 1989. A section of raised freeway and a bridge collapsed, crushing cars. Since 1989, freeways and public buildings have been strengthened.

▲ *The remains of San Francisco's buildings after the devastating 1906 earthquake.*

THE BIG ONE

Scientists think the next big earthquake will probably hit San Francisco and the surrounding areas before 2040. Experts estimate that an earthquake of the same magnitude as 1906 would kill two or three thousand people, injure many thousands more, damage 120,000 buildings and cost about 120 billion US dollars. The Big One could arrive now, or in ten years time. For any city in an earthquake zone, it's not a matter of if it will happen, but when.

GLOSSARY

aftershock an earthquake that happens after the main earthquake

ash tiny particles of solidified magma

avalanche a body of snow sliding down a hillside

conservative plate boundary a line along which the edges of two plates slide past each other

constructive plate boundary a line along which two tectonic plates are moving apart

core the central part of the Earth

crust the rocky top layer of the Earth

destructive plate boundary a line along which the edges of two tectonic plates are moving towards each other

earthquake wave a wave of energy that starts at the focus of an earthquake and passes through the rocks of the Earth

epicentre the point on the Earth's surface directly above an earthquake's focus

fault a crack in the rocks of the Earth's crust

focus the place in the Earth's crust where an earthquake happens.

foreshock a small earthquake that happens before the main earthquake

hazard map a map of an area showing areas that are likely to be affected by an earthquake

infrastructure the roads, railways, airports, water and energy supplies that allow a country to function

intensity the size of earth movements caused by an earthquake

landslide the sudden movement of rock and soil down a slope

liquefaction when soil behaves like a liquid during an earthquake, causing mudslides and allowing the foundations of buildings to sink

liquefy to turn from solid to liquid

magma molten rock underground

magnitude in the case of earthquakes, a measure of the size of earthquake waves

mantle the thick layer of rock between the Earth's core and the crust

masonry bricks, stone or concrete

molten melted

moment magnitude scale a scale that measures the energy of an earthquake

plate boundary the line along which two tectonic plates meet

Richter scale a scale that measures the magnitude (strength) of an earthquake

seismic to do with earthquakes or vibrations in the ground

seismologist someone who studies the internal structure of the Earth

seismometer an instrument that detects and measures earthquake waves

tectonic plate one of the huge pieces that makes up the Earth's lithosphere

tsunami a fast-moving wave at sea, set off by an earthquake under the ocean, or by a landslide

Further information

British Geological Survey
General information about earthquakes and up-to-date information on British earthquakes.
www.earthquakes.bgs.ac.uk

Discovery Channel
The Discovery Channel has many interesting videos relating to earthquakes.
www.discovery.com/video-topics/other/other-topics-earthquake-videos.htm

GeoHazards International
Global earthquake charity, with information on its work to prevent deaths during earthquakes, particularly those of school children.
www.geohaz.org/

United States Geological Survey
Information, news and photographs of earthquakes around the world.
www.earthquake.usgs.gov/

BBC
An interactive earthquake site from the BBC.
www.news.bbc.co.uk/1/hi/world/4126809.stm

Explore the BBC's archive of video clips relating to earthquakes.
www.bbc.co.uk/science/earth/natural_disasters/earthquake

GeoResources
A list of good weblinks about earthquakes.
www.georesources.co.uk/earthquake3.htm

NOTE TO PARENTS AND TEACHERS:
Every effort has been made by the Publishers to ensure that the websites in this book are suitable for children, that they are of the highest educational value, and that they contain no inappropriate or offensive material. However, because of the nature of the Internet, it is impossible to guarantee that the contents of these sites will not be altered. We strongly advise that Internet access is supervised by a responsible adult.

INDEX